Tabby Cats as Pets

A Complete Tabby Cats Owner's Guide

Tabby Cats General Info, Purchasing, Showing, Care, Cost, Diet, Health, Supplies, Grooming, Training and More Included!

By Lolly Brown

Foreword

You may have heard the term "tabby" cat but do you know exactly what breed is a tabby cat? What many people don't know is that tabby cats aren't actually a cat breed, it's a coat pattern. If somebody says "I have a tabby cat," they're sort of referring to a breed with a tabby coat. It has become sort of a catch – all term for cats. A tabby coat can be described as a coat with stripy markings but there's more to it than the general description.

So all in all, the word "tabby" describes a domestic cat's markings. It's not a breed. This only means that even if a tabby cat isn't a specific cat breed, a cat of a certain breed like a Maine Coon can still be called a tabby cat.

Now that you know what a tabby cat is, it's important to note that keeping them is nothing short of caring for any kind of cat breed. You have a responsibility to meet their basic needs and take good care of them.

This book will guide you on how you can properly care for your pet Tabby cat. You'll get to learn more about their biological information, training and grooming needs, health, and the proper diet to keep your pet healthy and happy!

Table of Contents

Welcome to the World of Tabby Cats!

According to a judge from the American Cat Fanciers Association (ACFA), a tabby pattern can be identified when the pigment of a cat's individual hair particularly in the hair shaft occurs in an alternate swaths or shades of light and dark color. Needless to say, if you have a cat that has a hair shaft filled with a solid pigment, then that cat is not a tabby – or doesn't have a tabby coat pattern. The tabby coat pattern can be found in any cat breed. There are actually three genes that are responsible for this outcome. These include Taqpep, Mc1R and the Agouti Signaling Protein (ASIP).

The ASIP gene is the factor that determines whether the coat of a cat will become banded or solid. The Mc1R gene, on the other hand, determines how light or dark the coat is going to be. According to the judge from ACFA, if the cat's ASIP gene is more dominant, then the pigment will be in bands particularly in the hair shaft which will create a tabby pattern in the breed. On the other hand, if a cat has two recessive non – ASIP gene, then the hair shaft will be solid and there will be no tabby pattern in a cat's coat.

The Taqpep tabby gene is in charge of the cat's pattern expression. According to Dr. Grahn, a forensic analyst from the Veterinary Genetics Laboratory at UC Davis, a kitten is born with a coat pattern that it will possess for the rest of its life.

There are actually four kinds of tabby patterns in cats. These are the classic tabby pattern, the ticked tabby pattern, the mackerel tabby pattern, and the spotted tabby pattern. Of these four types, the mackerel is the most common tabby pattern. It's usually the one that sports sort of like a tiger stripes on an orange tabby or a ginger tabby breed.

A common example is a Maine Coon cat. It sports a tiger – striped coat which is an example of mackerel tabby pattern. According to the judge from ACFA, the stripes on a mackerel tabby have a fishbone pattern that run in straight lines on the cat's body. You can also see that they sport a stripy pattern on their tails and legs, on the cheeks, and also a couple of stripes on their neck and under their chin. They also have that famous "M" shape stripe on their forehead and spots on their belly.

Classic tabbies have swirling stripes that are also wide. They also have a bull's eye shape on each side of their bodies and also a butterfly – shape across its shoulders. Classic tabby pattern also have a dark line that runs the length of the spine, an M – shaped stripes on their forehead as well as striped tails and legs.

There are actually a few myths about that "M" mark. Some people say that tabby cats are a gift from Mohammed, since he had one named Muzza. There's another one wherein a tabby cat is laying next to baby Jesus, and Mother Mary stroked the letter M onto the cat's forehead in gratitude.

Another famous breed with a tabby pattern is Abyssinian cats. They sport a ticked tabby pattern. Ticked tabby cats usually lack patterning on their bodies but they still have stripes on their head and legs.

Abyssinian cats are also sometimes referred to as sporting agouti hairs. They are the most common example of cat breed with ticked tabby pattern along with Singapura cats.

For spotted tabby cats, the Bengal cat is the most common example. Spotted tabby cats are exactly what they are: spotted. This kind of pattern shows up as spots on a cat's backs and sides; an example of blotched or spotted tabbies also includes the Egyptian Mau, Pixiebob, and Ocicat.

All four types of tabby patterns occur in various cat color patterns including but are not limited to blue, white, red, brown, chocolate and cream. According to the judge from AFCA, there are no relationship between a breed's markings and other physical traits such as their body size or their coat length.

It's quite common to talk about tabby cats as if they are a cat breed but as you now know, they are not. The word tabby only denotes a coat pattern and it doesn't represent a particular cat breed. This pattern is common to many cats. In the next few chapters, you'll learn more on how to care for these "tabby cats."

Welcome to the World of Tabby Cats!

Chapter One: Facts about Tabby Cats

Tabby cats are everywhere! You've most definitely seen it – more times that you can remember? You know what's weird? It's the fact that most people won't be able to recall exactly how many times they've seen it, simply because most of them don't pay any attention to them. This is because even if tabby cats are so widespread they don't really stand out. They do have distinctive markings, but people are just so used to seeing them and think that it's just another type of cat which is most probably why even if they do have distinctive markings, they just tend to leave a lasting impression.

And yet, these cats are just as unique and amazing on their own. In this chapter, you'll learn more facts about cats with a tabby pattern, some of which could be shocking to you, and could lead you to wanting a tabby kitty right away! Read on!

Facts about Tabby Cats

In this section, we'll learn some interesting facts about cats and kittens born with a tabby coat pattern. Some of these we've already discussed a bit earlier but we will delve deeper into those so that you'll have a full context of what these cats are all about.

Fact #1: Tabby Cats are NOT breed specific

As we've briefly discussed on the introduction of this book, tabby kitties and cats are non – breed specific. Most people got this wrong but it's perhaps the most essential thing you need to know if you want to own a tabby – coated cat.

You can find the tabby cat in various feline breeds including common domestic ones as well as some types of exotic designer breeds. A common example of a designer breed with a tabby coat is the Ocicat.

Fact #2: "Tabby – coated" cats are among the most popular type of cats

This can still be argued, but if you look at the stats (why would you? Anyway, I went ahead and did that), I found out that breeds like Maine Coons, Persians, Siamese and British Shorthair cats are among the top choices of pets all over the world. And they all have one trait in common – they have tabby coats!

The tabby pattern is also common not only in domestic cat breeds but also in feral type of kittens. It is really the most popular fur pattern among cats. Its commonness is perhaps why people don't pay much attention to Tabby kittens, but don't be deceived, because even if they aren't some kind of show – stoppers, it doesn't really mean they're not special or beautiful on their own. There's always something to appreciate about them, it just become so "normal" that we sometimes forget how distinct they are.

Fact #3: There are different types of Tabby markings

Did you know that there are various types of tabby markings? Yes! They come in different designs, so to speak. They come in stripes, lines, dots, and swirls as well as various other figures on their fur. How more diverse can they get?

Now don't confused this with what I've told you earlier wherein there are only four basic types of tabby cats; these four types are the "official standard tabby pattern." They're kind of like the flag carriers for the tabby pattern, so to speak.

Here are the four official type of the Tabby pattern:

- **Mackerel tabby** – the most common tabby pattern in cats

- **Classic tabby** – the blotched or marbled type with dark stripes as well as the M – shaped forehead mark.

- **Ticked tabby** – this is the pattern where there are no stripes (Abyssinian cats are the most common ticked tabby cat).

- **Spotted tabby** – this is pattern that comes with being spotted or patched.

Fact #4: Tabby cats have amazing eyes

The Oriental Shorthair is a breed that usually comes with the most colorful combinations. This cat sports an impressive patterns and hues (more than 300)! This type of feline is a fuzzy and colorful kitty mess BUT when it comes to eye color, tabby cats are the ultimate! Due to the fact that tabby – coated cats are found in various feline breeds, they can also display various eye shapes and eye colors depending on their genetic heritage and breed characteristics.

Fact #5: Tabby cats have wild looks but a domesticated personality

One of the many things that make Tabby cats amazing is that they have a nice temperament, which is cool because it's kind of contradictory; they can rock a wild cat look with a tame personality of a domesticated breed.

Designer cat breeders usually aim at producing litter with wild cat looks but can safely become a household pet. Tabby cats, regardless of their actual breed, mostly have that wild cat look even if they don't have a wild cat attitude. Another advantage of getting a tabby cat instead of an exotic designer feline breeds is that they are much cheaper and fun to keep.

Fact #6: Tabby cats have that mysterious "M" on their foreheads

Move aside, Harry Potter. Tabby cats can be easily recognized because most of them have a distinctive letter M on their foreheads. According to scientists, they have this because it is embedded in the kitten's DNA and most likely caused by the genes. However, they still can't prove where the tabby pattern originated from, or from what breed it came from which is why the M marking is just as mysterious as their origins. This paved the way for people to create myths around it. Here are some of them:

Christian Folklore

According to the legend, a tabby cat is curled up next to baby Jesus to keep him warm in his cradle. The Virgin Mary then stroked the cat's head as a sign of gratitude to the cat ad it left an M mark on the breed.

Islam Legend

It tells the tale of a tabby cat named Muezza. Apparently, Muezza save his master's life, the prophet Mohammed from a poisonous snake that had crawled up on his sleeve.

Egyptian Legend

The letter M is related to the word "mau" which literally translates to "cat" in the ancient Egyptian's language.

Due to the fact that tabby is a coat color that can be present in different feline breeds; tabby cats are diverse and just downright unique. Whether it's their personality, body structure, eye shape and color, playfulness, susceptibility to training or something else, you can expect to have a bit of everything from every tabby cat.

Fun Facts:

- Black and orange based tabby cats are also known as "marmalade cats"

- Morris is an orange tabby cat that starred as a commercial model for various cat – related products for many years

- Some people believe that tabby cats are the most favorite cats of those who are practicing witchcraft.

- Tabby cats have a life expectancy of around 10 to 15 years.

- Tabby cats with stripe pattern are also known as "tigers cats"

- The word tabby has various origins. Some people say that it came from the word Attabiy district in Baghdad which is a place where they sell patterned silks. In the 14th century, the word "atabis" was also used in France to refer to colored – marked cat breeds.

- Tabby cats are generally affectionate not just to their keepers but also to other animals

- Some of the most common purebred tabby cats include Bengals, British Shorthairs, Abyssinians, American Shorthairs and Maine Coons.

- Author and Professor Jim Willis had his own fiction story of how tabby cats have the letter M on their foreheads. He wrote a story about them as part of his book called Pieces of My Heart: Writings Inspired by Animals and Nature that was published in 2002.

- Orange tabby cats have develop little black freckles on their mouth and nose area. This is usually common around one to two years old.

- Tabby cats can grow up to around 16 inches in height. A particular example is the main coon tabby cat.

- Since most of the orange and ginger tabby cats are males, it can usually explain these cats' mischievous behaviors.

- Aside from common tabby cat names like Tiger, Morris and Garfield, tabby cats usually have names like Spot, Tabby and Marble.

Chapter Two: Buying Guide for Tabby Cats

Now that we've talked about how unique tabby cats really are, you might be wondering how much they cost. The best tip I can give you on how to get a tabby kitten or cat for less is to opt for shelters. You can also ask from your friends who may have a pregnant cat because most likely in a litter, there will be a tabby cat since it's the most widespread fur pattern, this is also true for animal shelters. In addition to that, if you acquire one from a shelter, you don't just get to save money, you also get to save a life.

Buying Guide for Tabby Cats

Here are some guidelines when it comes to the price range of a tabby cat:

- For captive – bred tabby cats: they can cost around $100 or less

- Purebred tabby cats: it can cost around $700 to $1,500

- Designer tabby breeds (like Bengal cats): these exotic felines can have a purchase price of $2,000 or more.

One of the reasons why tabby cats are great to keep as pets especially for first – time cat keepers is that they don't really have any specific health issues, although this will depend on where you acquire the kitten or how the tabby was raised.

Unlike the genetic albino cats, the tabby pattern doesn't carry any genetic heritage that's linked to a specific disease or other health kind of health issues. The health condition of a tabby cat and its susceptibility to common diseases or disorders will highly depend on the breed itself, its upbringing, environment, and diet. Whether your pet tabby will thrive and be healthy is totally up to the keeper, to you.

Famous Tabby Cats around the World

Just because tabby cats are common, it doesn't mean that they're not in any way special. As a matter of fact, there are lots of tabby cats that have left their mark in history. Below are some of the most famous tabby cats around the world.

Freya

Freya is the pet of UK's former Chancellor of Exchequer, George Osborne. The tabby cat Freya made it into the news many times over the past few years because she's quite known for her disappearing acts. She also loves bullying Osborne's other pet, a dog, to the extent that she was banned from Downing Street. Freya was sent to live in the isolated Kent countryside. Feisty freya!

Think Think and Ah Tsai

Think Think and Ah Tsai are two pet tabby cats owned by Tsai Ing – wen, Taiwan's president. We can probably say that they are the "First Cats." Think Think is a female tabby with a grey coat. Prior to being given as a gift to President Tsai Ing – Wen, she was actually a rescue. Ah

Tsai, on the other hand, is a male tabby cat with a ginger coat. He was also given as a gift to the President by a friend during the presidential campaign. Both of these tabby cats have appeared numerous times in the news and social media.

Garfield

Speaking of famous, this list wouldn't be complete without mentioning the most famous tabby of them all – Garfield! He's an adorable cat who's self – centered, and one of the well – known movie cartoon characters of all time.

Oscar and Miko

Now we go to the Queen – the band, not the Queen, queen. I'm talking about Queen's lead vocalist, Freddy Mercury. He has lots of cats, and two of them are tabby cats. Both of them were actually rescued along with many others, which is most probably given to him as gifts, or also rescued from shelters.

David Bowie's Tabby Cats

It seems like famous rockers have a soft – heart for tabby cats. Another famous musician, David Bowie, not only has cats but also wrote songs about the feline breed. He even attended a photo shoot of an Abyssinian tabby cat!

Toby

Betty White, famous actress and comedienne in Hollywood, once had an orange colored tabby cat named Toby. According to her, Toby helped her developed a love for animals in general. White is also a well – known animal activist with over 40 years of humanitarian work done for different organizations that's fighting for animal rights and welfare.

Mark Twain's Tabby Cats

Another famous historical figure whose love for tabby kitties did not go unnoticed is none other than Mark Twain. According to various sources, Twain not only surrounded himself with kitties, he also had a tabby pet that was quite special to him. Rumor has it that he's played pool with a his tabby cat.

Heathcliff

Heathcliff, just like Garfield, is an orange tabby cat. He's a famous fiction character that didn't just gained worldwide popularity through his own comic strip, but also through the two animated TV series produced in the 1980s. Heathcliff also starred on a theater movie. Due to the cat's striking looks, hilarious pranks and mischief, he gained a huge fan base back in the days.

Oliver

Oliver is included in the main characters in the animation called Oliver & Company. He's also an orange tabby kitten whose unlikely temperament helps him befriends dogs and later helps him save his owner's life.

Tiger

Another popular tabby cat who made history with his uniqueness because of his unnatural behavior is known as Tiger. He's a long – haired tabby cat that starred in the animation called An American Tail. Guess what? He's a vegan!

Maru

Maru is a Scottish Fold tabby cat that went viral a few years back. He's one of the most popular cats on Youtube. In fact, his videos have been viewed over 300 million times!

Now that's what you call #TabbyTrend

Lil Bub

Lil Bub is another internet celebrity tabby cat that's also an animal activist, a meme inspiration and even an author! Lil Bub has actually raised more than $300,000 over the years for many animals who are in need of help and love.

Cheshire Cat

Who can forget the ever – puzzling Cheshire cat? Even if this tabby has changed her appearance throughout the decades (from grey to green to blue to purple and more), his stripes are his main feature along with his shining pearly whites.

Loki

Loki, no not the one from Avengers, is another famous tabby cat in Instagram. This tabby cat is famous for its mischievous expressions and vampire – like appearance. He's been followed on Instagram by around 350,000 followers and counting.

As you can see, tabby cats aren't only popular in shelters, and in movies or literature, they are also popular among famous keepers. Tabby cats are diverse in terms of physical traits and temperament; they can make great feline companions even if they don't really grab your attention at first sight.

If you think you are ready to welcome a Tabby cat as part of your family, make sure to visit your local shelters. Chances are you will find a tabby cat right where you are, the question is you ready to handle these feisty, and adorable creatures.

Chapter Three: How Can I Own a Tabby?

When it comes to acquiring one, finding a good breeder is what you need to do to be paired with a healthy Tabby. Reputable breeders follow a code of ethics prohibiting sales to wholesalers and pet stores. The code they observe and abide outlines the breeder's responsibilities to buyers and their breeds. To find breeders and to get more information about the personality and history of the Tabby you can check out cat association websites like the Cat Fanciers Association, and the American Cat Fanciers Association.

This chapter will provide you with information on how you can legally keep this rare and treasured breed as well as some tips on how to find the right breeder.

Cat Laws for Keepers

Cats are becoming a staple member of households and even private institutions all over the world, which make the presence of laws governing cat ownership essential. Ultimately, laws are geared towards protecting pets from abuse and neglect as well as protecting the community from animals that may become threatening to the public. As responsible pet owners, it is our duty to be fully informed about them and uphold them. By doing so, we are contributing to a better community not only for our feline friends, but also for ourselves.

Unlike dog owners, cat owners are not required to obtain a license for their cats across all states in the U.S., except in Rhode Island, where it is mandated. However, there are some municipal ordinances that may require proof of vaccination and identification, particularly in Alabama, where owners are required to have their cat or dog vaccinated yearly to make sure that all pets, owners, and civilians are protected from rabies. This is actually a good measure in the event of cat bites and scratches. Remember, cats can be infected with rabies, too, so if you haven't yet, bring your pet to a vet and ask to be scheduled for vaccination as soon as possible.

Cats are not required to wear collars in the U.S. as it is believed to go against their nature. It is, however, good for cats get used to wearing collars so that they can be easily identified in the event that your cat accidentally gets out the gate and gets lost, having the owner's contact details on the collar makes is easier for concerned citizens to help out, and so that people can be informed of the cat's medical condition. This comes in handy particularly if you're leaving your cat in a pet inn while you're away on a trip.

To ensure that your cat's collar won't interfere with its movements or cause injuries, always check if it is properly secured on the neck. If you can slip two fingers between the collar and the kitty's neck, then it's all good! A collar that's too tight might cause irritation, while having it too loose might cause it to get snagged on objects.

It is highly advisable to have their collar inscribed with any medical conditions they have to ensure that your cat will be properly fed and cared for. Same goes for when your cat goes missing; people who found it would immediately know that the cat needs special medical attention. For further information regarding licensing requirements and ordinances in your area, you can give your local government a call or simply look up their website, ask or check if there are downloadable forms for cat licensing, mail the form to the town hall or hand it over personally. The registration fee may vary across the states.

If you live in the United Kingdom, your cat may be required to undergo a quarantine period as a strict safety measure. They definitely love their feline friends so much that earlier this year, the government pledged to develop more laws to protect kittens from exploitation. This was after discovering that some kittens are being bred in poor conditions and are taken away from their mothers too soon. The new law states that license exemptions for people who repeatedly sell kittens that are bred from non - pedigree cats will be removed, and there will be stricter conditions for breeder licenses to be approved.

Sources for Tabby Cats

Unhealthy catteries and disreputable breeders can be difficult to identify from reliable operations. There is no absolute guarantee that you won't be purchasing an ill kitten. Therefore asking the right questions, researching the breed so you understand what to expect and visiting the facilities to determine the conditions and see the animals for yourself is vital to lessen the chances of heartache, disappointment and wasted finances.

Make sure that you have a clean contract with your source (clearly stating the responsibilities of both breeder and buyer), or you have the necessary permits if you're going to acquire one from a rescue group or shelter. Whether you get a kitten or adult Tabby, you will need to take your kitten or cat to the veterinarian right after adoption. Your veterinarian will be able to see problems with the feline's health, and would work with you to create a preventive regimen which will help avoid countless health issues.

Prior to buying a kitten, think about whether a mature Tabby might be a better choice for you and your lifestyle. Kittens are buckets full of fun but they also entail a load of work and could be somewhat destructive until they reach a more easy-going state of adulthood. If you purchase an adult, you would know more about what to expect of the cat in terms of health and personality. Should you consider getting an adult Tabby instead of a kitten, ask breeders about buying a retired breeding or a show cat. Check out the previous chapter about the pros and cons of getting a kitten versus an adult cat.

Rescue No More

There are many reasons why adult pets end up in shelters and rescue facilities like divorce, death, owners relocated, illness and the list goes on. You might stumble onto good fortune and find the perfect Tabby for you and your family. You could also try checking your shelters in your locale or check out pet finder listings.

Selecting the wrong breeder can make or break you as a pet keeper. If you acquire your Tabby from an illegitimate source, you may eventually find out that the kitten you got is not even a Tabby! Since this breed is expensive, rare and one of a kind, you need to make sure that you only get it from a reputable source. However, breeders aren't the only source to acquire a Tabby cat. You won't usually find a Tabby kitten in rescues or shelters but you may still come across both mixed and pedigreed Tabby breeds there.

No matter where you get your Tabby pet make sure that there is a written contract with the seller, shelter or rescue group is thorough and details the responsibilities of both parties. If you look up this breed online you will get quite a few hits on breeders selling. It can be daunting to figure out which breeders are reputable and which ones are just in it for the money. Things like convenience, such as ability to pay online, multiple kitten availability at all times, having choices for any kitten "readily available" are some of the red flags that would identify a shady "breeder" because after all Tabby is a rare breed.

Select a breeder who has completed the health certifications required to screen out genetic health problems to the fullest extent possible. You need to get in touch with a breeder who raises and keeps the kittens in their home. Isolated kittens can become skittish, fearful and may be difficult to socialize later. Run away from breeders who only seem bent in how fast they can pass on and unload a kitten on you. Turn your back on those who are more concerned about whether your credit card will go through. You also want to be able to pay a visit to their home facilities and check out with your own eyes how they interact and how the kittens respond to them.

Reputable breeders will have no problems welcoming you into their premises. Buying from a website with no possibility of seeing the pets in action leaves you very little guarantee that you will be getting what was agreed upon. This is why we highly recommend that you check the cat personally and not just through online photos or videos.

You can also pay a visit and discuss this with your veterinarian. They can usually point you to the direction of a breed rescue organization, a reputable breeder, or other trustworthy sources of healthy kittens. Put as much effort into researching your kitten as you would into picking out a new car or other big ticket purchases. Doing so will save you money in the long run. Depending on what pet you are looking for, you may have to sit it out for six months or more before the right kittens are available. So be patient. Reputable breeders typically will not hand over kittens to new people until the kittens are between twelve and sixteen weeks of age.

Chapter Four: Turf for Your Tabby Cats

The environment greatly impacts a cat's overall health and behavior, which is why both the U.S. and U.K. gave reminders and recommendations regarding setting up the right environment for cats, specifically the amount of space needed, the furniture, interaction with other pets and with their owners or other people as well as environmental enrichment including toys and other sensory stimulants.

You see, cats are fairly comfortable living on their own, and unlike dogs, they would rather keep a distance to avoid social conflicts. If you want to set up the right environment for your Tabby you need to keep in mind of some things like providing an adequate hiding spot and cat essentials as well as providing a secure playing area that's safe from hazards.

You have to make sure that there will be hiding spots where your pet can seek refuge and be out of sight at times when it feels stressed or uncomfortable with interactions. You need to provide litter trays, water bowl, and food bowls and make it easily accessible for him/ her especially if you're going to leave your cat. In case you have more than one pet at home, give each pet their own bowls with sufficient supply of food to avoid monopolization.

One thing that keeps a cat happy is when it knows that it has a safe and comfortable home. Sometimes though, a cat's curious nature gets it into trouble, creating a hassle both for you and your pet. More mature cats are less likely to be mischievous, while kittens can be a bit trickier to handle. Whatever the size of your home is, you will definitely need to ensure that it is cat - proof and an ideal place for your feline friend to thrive. For sure you've seen tons of entertaining videos all over social media showing a tiny cat comfortably sleeping on a mini bed tailor - made for it. Although it looks absolutely adorable, kittens will need more than just cozy sleeping furniture to grow healthy and strong. This chapter will teach you tips and tricks to ensure that your home is ready for the arrival of your Tabby cat.

Reminders on the Ride Home and Upon Arriving

Bringing home a new pet could be a really special experience for humans, but for cats, it can be quite frightening. For you to be able to help them feel secure and ease their tension, you must first understand why cats are scared when being re - homed. Cats dislike change; for them, a new home means entering new territory, meeting new possible enemies, and encountering new challenges they are not all too familiar with.

Make sure that your Tabby cat is inside a carrier to that it feels safer. Being inside moving vehicles may traumatize your cat and cause it much stress that it would start to pant. Panting is a sure sign of anxiety and excessive body heating, so help your cat by keeping it safe inside a well - ventilated cat carrier.

Upon arriving home, it is advised that you let your cat settle into a small room that he can call his early territory. Never force the cat out of the carrier, instead, keep it open and let the cat decide when it is comfortable enough to explore the room. You can have your cat stay in the room for several days so that he gets used to the smells, the sounds, and the sights. Put everything the cat needs in this room, including water and food bowls, litter tray, a few toys to keep him busy, and a comfortable bedding.

You may visit the cat often to see if it is doing fine, but don't stress it out by giving it forced attention or by bringing in new people to the room to pet or play with the cat. Also see to it that your kids don't frighten the cat by entering their haven uninvited. Most cat breeds including the Tabby are known to easily adapt to its environment, but letting them get used to their new home and new human companions at their own pace will work wonders on your relationship with them.

Avoid Cat Fights

One of the most common conflicts among cats is guarding their resources from each other, but this may be avoided if you properly allocate their needs. Another important factor is to maximize the vertical space by incorporating elevated and vertical structures inside your house such as climbing poles, shelves, slanted walkways, steps, platforms, cat hammocks, cat trees, resting boxes and the likes since the Tabby cats are born climbers and jumpers. You don't need all of the things aforementioned, but having at least some of these in your house is highly essential when living with a cat.

One thing more difficult than introducing a new cat to humans is introducing it to other pets because it's not easy controlling animal behavior, much less, decoding their thoughts and understanding what they're trying to say. You can expect that one pet of yours will always try to dominate your new cat, as animals are territorial in nature. Give them time to meet the new member of the family and extend your patience and trust the process.

An older cat is likely to accept another adult cat much easier than it is to like new kittens at once. It will be best to separate the resident cats from the new cat upon arrival, so that you can manage their initial encounter. If you have more than one resident cat at home, introduce them to the new cat individually. It's not necessary to have the cats spend time together immediately.

When it comes to introducing your cat to your dog/s, keep in mind that meeting a resident dog may be a scary experience for your Tabby cat. We highly recommend that you keep your dog confined or in a leash upon the arrival of the new cat. Make sure that the cat's initial base is not accessible to the dog to prevent it from cornering of chasing the cat, even if it only wants to play. Do not let your dog frighten the cat by showing signs of aggression or intimidating the cat by barking. Give your cat and dog enough time to get to know each other by not forcing interaction. Do not leave them alone together unsupervised if you are not sure yet whether they like each other or not.

Make sure to keep the cat in its temporary room until it feels confident enough to roam around. Keep an eye out for when your cats see each other for the first time. Make sure that they keep a distance to prevent aggression, as first impressions indeed last. And if there will be no signs of hostility among the cats in the coming days, you may now let them spend time together without a worry.

Do You Need a Cat Sitter?

Should you plan to travel with your Tabby cat then you may need to consider some things before you even pack your pet with you. This holds true especially if you do not want to leave your precious pet with a cat sitter. Taking your pet to another place is time - consuming and complicated process which is why you should do extensive research before you go through the process.

If you are only going away for a short period of time, it's probably best to entrust your pet to your family or friends. Tabby cats can be left alone provided that you already trained them and you leave them with all the essentials they need such as food, water, toys, security etc. They are independent and they can survive for quite some time without you. However, if you are going to be gone for a long period of time (few weeks, months to a year) then it's best to bring them along with you.

Do you think your pet will be all right to be in a confined place for a long period of time? Make sure to make them comfortable during the whole trip whether it's by car, on the air or at sea. It's also important to check with the airline or shipping line with regards to their regulations on bringing a pet on board.

Some airlines may allow pets to travel in the cabin, only if you have a small cage that will fit under your seat while some airlines will restrict the pet transportation during certain times of the year. Research on the air pressure and temperature in the cargo before you book the flight. It is better for your pet if your flight is direct and has a short travel time. Make sure to research on the specific requirements for the airlines or shipping lines when it comes to transportation of the pet. Before the travel, make sure you have trained your cat to be inside the crate or kennel. You can add toys and pieces of clothing so your pet will be very familiar during the transportation. Last but not least, find pet-friendly airlines or pet – friendly shipping lines before you book your trip.

Turf Essentials

Felines prefer to spend more time in high places, and having them navigate through these structures will surely be a good exercise and entertainment for them.

You need to also keep containers closed at all times. Kittens are naturally curious and are more likely to climb whatever structures they can. It is a must to keep water containers, garbage cans, and washers & dryers closed at all times as cats can get trapped inside when they fall.

Also bear in mind that an open toilet bowl could attract thirsty kittens and may cause drowning, so protect your feline friends by keeping those lids closed. Of course, a home is not complete if you do not provide comfortable bedding in ideal resting areas. Cats in general enjoy resting in dry and warm areas, usually in corners where they feel more secure. Try to get creative and make cat beds from soft materials such as polyester fleece cloth, so you wouldn't need to spend much on new beds. Studies show that cats that sleep on soft surfaces tend to rest longer than those who sleep on hard surfaces.

Another thing to keep in mind is to not encourage your cat to nap near hot surfaces like stoves or fireplaces. Although they enjoy resting in warm areas, the fireplace and kitchen top are absolutely not safe places for rest. Gently wake up your cat and move it to a safer spot to remind them that these are not the correct places for napping.

When it comes to essentials, make sure to allot one litter tray for your pet. This is also the ideal allocation if you have several cats at home to ensure good toilet behavior. Remember that cleaning the litter box at least once per day is a must because some cats won't use a tray that's been soiled. You'll find a variety of cat litter in the groceries, and it may take some experimenting to know which type is the most ideal for your cat. Also keep in mind that the locations of the litter box and feeding bowls must be at least 0.50 meters apart and not be interchanged to prevent confusion.

Never leave hazardous and poisonous chemicals exposed. Cats are curious and playful in nature. They will tinker with almost every object they come across with, and you wouldn't want you cat suddenly knocking over that bottle of bleach or detergent, or worse, accessing roach and rodent killers. Make sure to keep all dangerous substances secured in cabinets with locks. It's also best to keep away toxic plants at home. Not all plants can be used as catnip, some turn out to be harmful to cats. The most common toxic houseplants are lilies, poinsettia Philodendron, and mistletoe. While garden plants that you should keep your cat away from are daffodils and azaleas.

Do not leave cords and strings dangling. Both adult cats and kittens love chewing and playing with things they can reach or find on the ground. The problem is getting badly entangled in these wires could cause choking. Make sure tape and secure electrical wiring properly. Kittens may think wires are fun to play with, but one wrong bite on this and they'll end up getting badly hurt or electrocuted, and may even cause electrical problems in your home. Avoid problems by checking the house for loose wirings before bringing in a new pet. Don't scatter items like hair ties, rubber hands, ribbons, cable ties, rubber erasers, thread, yard, small toy pieces, doll accessories etc.

One way of making sure that your Tabby does not play around hazardous materials is to ensure that you provided physically and mentally stimulating cat toys to keep them busy. Tabby is known for their intelligence. They easily learn how to open doors, press buttons, and so much more that could get them into trouble. Giving your cat some toys would keep it busy and entertained.

Tabby Turf 2.0

Once you've got the furniture ready for your pet's arrival, it's now time to know how you can enhance the quality of your cat's life under your watch. Having an ideal house arrangement for pet cat is only the tip of the iceberg because as an owner, you'll need to plan their enrichment activities. Just like humans, pets can get easily bored as well. Playtimes commonly happen after their naps, and this is a good time to stimulate their brain through interaction and physical activities. Check out some tips below:

- **Set a little hammock or platform for your cat by the window to excite their eyes.** Most cats enjoy looking out windows and observing other people and animals. You can also try letting your Tabby cat explore your garden, but only if you are there to supervise him/ her. You wouldn't want to chase them through the neighborhood, so make sure that your gates are closed and never let your cat out of your sight.

- **If you're ever tried listening to classical music, you'd know how effective it can be as a stress reliever – cats included!** Some say that it has the same effects on cats and other household pets. Although it hasn't been proven, there's no harm in playing soothing music for your Tabby cat whenever you see it being hyper active or agitated. Certain types of sounds stimulate their auditory senses. It is highly likely for cats to enjoy music that mimic the rhythm and tonal qualities of purrs. However, the type of music we usually like is definitely not the type they enjoy, so be sensitive to your pet before deciding to blast music from your speakers. It hasn't been determined yet whether cats prefer high-pitched or low-pitched sounds. Generally speaking, extremely loud noise could be harmful to your cat.

- **Catnip is absolutely safe for cats, but feeding them too much of this may cause diarrhea or vomiting.** To avoid habituation, it's recommended that you don't give catnip more than once every two to three weeks. Catnip is readily available in pet supplies stores, along with toys stuffed with it. Olfactory stimulation should also be on your priority as cats are born with a highly - developed sense of smell. If you can observe, cats immediately react to certain smells as they get easily attracted by the scent of deliciously - cooked food, and they instantly back away from people, food, or objects whose scent they don't like or recognize. You can help enhance their sense of smell by providing posts or surfaces for scratching. This is especially helpful when you have more than one cat at home as cats communicate via their scent glands.

- **Meal time is every pet's most loved daily activity.** Full and satisfied cats are happy cats as they sleep more soundly and behave better when they are not deprived of a good meal. Since cats like the Tabby breed are natural hunters, letting them perform natural feeding behaviors could greatly stimulate their appetite and even their brain functions. In the wild, cats hunt often and they end up eating ten small meals daily.

- **Food puzzle toys enables cat to figure out how to work the object in order to get its food.** You can provide treat balls wherein the cat has to roll the ball until cat food falls from the tiny holes all over the ball. You can make one at home by cutting holes on small containers, water bottles, or even toilet paper roles, and then, putting dry food inside it. Your cat will surely be intrigued by the sound the treats make when it moves the container.

- **Another type of food puzzle will not only allow cats to experience natural feeding behaviors is known as foraging feeders.** It can also help prevent cats from over indulging that leads to obesity. It mimics the experience of scooping out food from small, difficult spaces, which cats in the wild usually do. You can also play circuit boards which is a type of food puzzle toy was initially created for animals kept in zoos or in laboratories for observation. Cats simply manipulate objects in the circuit board in order to get their food. You can either buy ready-made boards or make one yourself.

You see each cat is unique and special in its own way, and sometimes they can get unpredictable. By doing your part as an owner, you are eliminating possible causes of behavior problems for house cats, such as frustration, boredom, and stress.

Not a lot of cat owners know how important it is to stimulate cats mentally and physically, and so they, too, become problematic when their pet cat starts destroying furniture, being loud or vocal at night, being aggressive, or worse, getting sick. All of these things can be avoided by being aware of your cat's need to express their natural behaviors. The amount of time a cat will finally feel comfortable in its new home varies according to its past experiences and personality. Giving a cat ample time to adjust to a new home will be beneficial both for you and your pet.

Chapter Five: Requirements for Tabby Kittens

Just like adult cats, kittens have their own specific needs too including a place to sleep, bowls to eat in, and fun time. Preparing these before their arrival will save you much time and effort. It will also allow you to find the best ones for them with your budget. You see, any type of pet you intend to keep will definitely cost you additional expenses. However, the price to pay is usually no match for the happiness of owning a pet. Tabby cats are low maintenance, but that doesn't mean you can maintain them without extra effort! As a responsible pet owner, it is your task to know the ideal environment for this breed to keep them feeling happy and secure in your home.

Tabby Kittens

Kittens in general are cute, charming, and need lots of care and attention. It can be compared to raising a toddler. It's a much bigger responsibility if you choose to acquire a kitten because you will need to train them, provide them with the vaccines they need, and socialize them well enough so that they will grow up to be well – mannered adult cats.

There could be a lot more responsibility when you acquire a kitten but it will surely be a rewarding experience because you will get to see him/ her grow, you'll be a part of your cat's life, and will become more bonded as the years go by.

Kittens are easier to train and socialize, whether you will train it to use a litter box or teach them various tricks. They are also less prone to trouble as they will not get tangled in cods, fall from high places, or be as curious as an adult cat. Kittens are generally easier to introduce to people, fellow cats, or other household pets. Having kittens can also be beneficial to your health and emotional well - being. It can lower your blood pressure and cholesterol. Getting kittens could teach you and your little children about daily responsibility, because there are a lot of things you need to take care of kittens.

In addition to this, kittens can help you in your social life as they can pave the way in establishing new connections with fellow pet owners within your area.

As for the disadvantages, if you get a very young kitten, you may need to bottle feed it. You will also need to get all the vaccines and booster shots throughout its first year which can be both expensive and time – consuming.

Kitty Kit

In this section, you'll learn the things your Tabby kitten needs including some kitty essentials. Make sure to prepare them before your new kitten arrives

Cat patios are structures that provide protection for your cat especially if they are staying outdoors. This is a perfect solution for your cat to enjoy the sights and sounds of the world outside while keeping it safe. If you're having second thoughts about allowing your cat outdoors, building a cat patio will provide the "outside world" that it needs.

In addition to that it will also provide benefits such as reduction of veterinary bills due to contracted illnesses and injuries from the outdoors, and it will also give your cat a healthier lifestyle because it can do sunbathing, watch birds, have exercise opportunities, and inhale fresh air. Cat patios also lessen indoor odors by providing another litter box in the enclosure and it can also help reduce the free - roaming cat population in the neighborhood.

Setting up an enclosure entails your time, effort, and additional costs. You can either hire a builder and designer, or you can Do – It – Yourself (DIY). You can check available supplies with your local hardware store and start building.

Find a spot that you cat can easily access like a door, an existing window or a patio where you can build a cat door. You need to also make sure that the location you choose won't be too warm because exposure to direct sunlight during the hottest periods of the day could be harmful to your Tabby. You also need to be able to access the enclosure for cleaning and maintenance purposes.

Make sure to consider the age and condition of your pet. This will help you decide what type of furniture you need to install in the enclosure. Ramps are also ideal for Tabby cats. Bigger or more elaborate enclosures could look nice, but keep in mind that you'll be having other expenses for food, grooming, supplies, and vet visits which mean you need to consider your budget so that you won't blow all of it on an enclosure.

Any kitten or cat will absolutely like anything soft. You may opt for a pillow or a cat bed. Consider the size of your cat when buying bedding. A bed that is too large might leave your pet feeling unsettled. On the other hand, a bed that is too small will ultimately be uncomfortable. As for the cat furniture, you should provide scratch posts or pads, cat trees or something that can provide an outlet for their jumping instincts. These types of furniture will allow your cat to express their natural behaviors such as leaving marks on their territory and climbing. Costs depend on the type you want, but cat furniture prices usually start at around $20 while the price of bedding may vary depending on the size, quality, brands, or design you prefer.

The best type of bowls especially if you acquired a Tabby kitten is the shallow ones because it allows easy access to their food and water. There are many types of bowls to choose from, and plastic is the most popular. However, this material is known to retain smells that the cat may find foul and may discourage them from finishing their food. In some cases, cats that are allergic to plastic end up having a type of cat acne on their chin. The most recommended type of food bowl is stainless steel because it is sturdy and generally harmless for cats. Steel bowls are often dishwasher safe, which could help busy owners save time.

Make sure to keep the food bowls clean and rinse them regularly to prevent the build-up of bacteria. It will cost you around $3 for a single bowl and around $6 for a set of 2 bowls. Depending on your cat's personality, you can either choose a hooded litter box from privacy or a plain plastic tray for those who don't enjoy feeling boxed. Cats tend to do their potty business in the same areas, unlike dogs that need to be walked until they find an ideal area. This is why you need to get your cat a litter box.

There a lot of types if litter boxes depending on your budget and your preferences. There is even an automated poop handler that could do the dirty work for you. There are various types of cat litter such as clumping and non – clumping clay, wheat, recycled paper, grass, corn – based litter, walnut shells (crushed), gel crystals to name a few. The most common type of litter available in the groceries is clumping-cat litter; it is highly - absorbent, although it tends to be a bit dusty. The cost of cat litter usually starts at $15.

You need to also make sure that you maintain your cat's litter box. What you can do is fill it up with about 2 to 3 inches so that your pet can dig through it and learn to cover its waste. Make sure to scoop out the waste at least twice a day. Some cats would not use a soiled litter box so in order to prevent them from doing their business elsewhere, ensure to keep their litter tray clean. Dispose the soiled litter properly by putting it in an appropriate garbage bag. Avoid using their poop as fertilizer because it will surely attract other cats, flies, insects etc.

Stock up on toys so that you and your family can bond with your pet. Playtime is very important for a kitten's development and it can be therapeutic for humans too. You can buy any type of cat toy you wish, just remember to avoid buying those with parts than can cause choking or strangling. There are a lot of cheap cat toys in the stores and online, so you don't have to worry about spending much on them. What you can do is to get a couple of them and rotate it so that your cat will not get bored easily with it. It's also best to consider what kind of toy your pet prefers.

Spaying and Neutering

When it comes to spaying and neutering your pet, vets strongly suggest that owners spay or neuter their cats. Neutering is found to have a lot of benefits including the correction of bad behavior such as territorial spraying, aggression, and roaming, which are common for male cats. Female cats can also be observed to have better behavior after surgery. If they are spayed between three to six months, you could protect them from mammary cancer and from an infection of the uterus which usually affects older female cats.

Operations at full - service vet clinics may cost you around $200 for a male cat, and $300 up to $500 for a female cat at the time of this writing. For non - profit spay or neuter services, they could charge as low as $50, and may vary according to your location. Only licensed veterinarians are allowed to perform these surgeries. You can check out the website of The American Society for the Prevention of Cruelty to Animals and Humane Society because they list low-cost spays and neuter programs for owners' reference.

Grooming Your Tabby

Proper grooming is essential in order to maintain your Tabby's coat, and overall well-being. Although cats in general can clean themselves well, you still have to take them on trips to a trusted groomer to make sure that they are in top shape.

If you want to maintain your pet's coat, you should comb and not just brush it by running your fingers through its coat to prevent matting. The coat will depend on the breed of the tabby cat you have.

Part of grooming practices is to check your pet's ear for foul odor and dirt build-up. They can usually clean this area by themselves, but you can help them by using a damp cotton ball and gently rubbing inside to collect dirt and debris. A cat with clean ears is a healthy cat. In addition to bathing, brushing its teeth is also important. Consult with a vet for your cat's dental health.

All breeds of cats are susceptible to dental problems, but you can minimize the risk of acquiring it with regular brushing. Last but not least is nail – trimming. You need to trim your Tabby's nails as this will prevent your cat from accidentally wounding both you and other animal companions. It can also help prevent damage on your home furniture. If you are not confident trimming its nails yourself, you may take your pet to a groomer and have it done there to avoid wounding its paws.

Chapter Six: Tabby Coat Mutations

Let's say you are new to cat keeping. Perhaps you've already bought your first cat for showing or breeding. If that's the case, then you've already started your education when it comes to identifying different coat colors and patterns/ markings among various pedigreed felines. On the other hand, if you haven't made the purchase yet, then worry not as this chapter will help you identify colors and patterns you may see as you start searching for your first tabby cat.

When it comes to describing your tabby cat's coat, the color and markings usually refer to exactly those elements or physical feature. The coat is the fur of your pet tabby, and this is obviously where you can see the animal's pattern and color as well as the coat length (shorthair or long – hair).

The coat colors don't suggest the breed or pedigree of a cat. For instance, Tabby is a pattern not a breed. This is also true for Albino cats, Tortoiseshell, Calico and the likes, all of which is a cat pattern not a breed.

How do we describe a coat color?

Color and pattern are the most common way to describe the pedigree of a show cat. There are actually two ways to describe the coat color – what it looks like and what cat experts call it. For instance, breeders and geneticists alike refer to a cat that's gray in color as a "blue cat." There are experts that call an orange – coated cat as a "red cat," for yellow or beige – colored coats; they refer to is as a "cream – colored cat."

There are many names for cats that sport a solid brown coat. They can be called as chocolate, sepia, sable or chestnut. For those who have a lavender – colored coat, they can be refer to as lilac, frost, platinum or lavender; the term will depend on the breed.

As for black cats and white cats, its name is as ease, unless of course you are referring to an ebony Oriental Shorthair, which is also a black cat.

What about Stripes?

Most of the time, a color doesn't describe a cat breed though naming the pattern can definitely helpful. There are various patterns that occur in the domesticated cat; this includes tabby, solid, pointed, parti – color and bi – color. Other characteristics such as the smoke and shaded effects are also useful when it comes to describing cats.

A cat breed that only has one color and doesn't have any white spots, or any form of tabby pattern is referring to a solid – colored felines. If for instance, a cat is black, you can refer to it as black, solid colored cat while a cream – colored cat can be referred to as cream, solid color, so on and so forth. There are various solid colors, these are the following:

- White
- Blue
- Lilac or lavender
- Cinnamon
- Chocolate
- Sable or brown
- Cream
- Red

A striped cat or a tabby cat has four patterns, and we've talked about this in previous chapters. These are classic, mackerel, ticked and spotted.

- The mackerel pattern is actually the most common tabby pattern. It can be described as a pattern where the stripes are narrow and runs parallel to one another just like a fish bone which is why it's known as mackerel.

- The classic tabby or blotched patter is where there are elaborate swirls and butterflies on the cat's sides and shoulders.

- The spotted tabby is sort of like a classic or mackerel pattern except that the swirls or stripes seem to be broken into spots of color.

- For ticked tabby cats, it usually appears as multiple bands of color on each hair. It can be found all over the cat's body particularly in the head, limbs and tail. This is also referring to as an agouti tabby pattern. Abyssinian cats are the best example.

If a cat is silver, blue, or brown tabby and has patches of cream or red, then that is considered as a "patched tabby." The patching seen in these cases are usually related to a sex – linked orange gene which is why it's usually seen in female felines.

No matter what tabby pattern is present in a domesticated cat there are usually intricate markings that can be found on its face. These are known as mascara markings. Mascara markings highlight the eyes and it usually traces their way across its face.

In addition to these, tabby cats also show bars or stripes on their limbs, their tummy area, and also in their spine – line, down the center of the cat's back and rings around their tails.

Each tabby cat also has distinctive M markings on their forehead, making the easier to identify. Elaborately marked tabby cats also have butterflies and bracelet patterns across their necks and shoulders.

For many people, tabby colors are one of the most difficult coat colors to learn. A brown tabby has a bronze or warm brown tone to his its background color and black stripes. For blue tabby cats, it has a creamy background color and blue stripes, while for a cream tabby; it has a light beige colored background with darker shade of beige stripes.

You might be wondering, why they don't just call the brown tabby a black tabby since it is its genetic description. Mostly it's out of habit and convention but it can also because brown tabby better describes its color.

Other kinds of tabby colors like the silver tabby which is a silver – white background color with black tabby markings that can either be a red tabby, cinnamon tabby, blue tabby, lilac tabby, cream tabby, chestnut tabby, and cameo tabby.

Pattern Designations

Parti – Colored Cats

A parti – colored coat is a cat that has more than one color present. Included in this parti – colored coat are the following:

- Tabby
- White
- Blue cream
- Calico
- Tortoiseshell
- Lavender
- Cream
- Bi - color

In the parti – color classification, there are various colors and patterns that are sex – linked orange gene. For instance, a tortoiseshell is a black chocolate while a seal – colored female has patches of red throughout its coat. A blue cream is a blue feline that has patches of cream, while a lavender cream cat is female lavender with cream

patches as well. Both the tortoiseshell and the lavender –
cream or blue can be augmented with color white. The
calico cat is a female with white and large solid areas of
black and red, blue and cream, as well as lilac and cream.

Bi – Colored Cats

A bi – color is also a parti – colored cat but they
have solid areas of white and another color or marking
like a tabby pattern. The usual colors of the bi – colored
cat include red and white, blue and white, black and
white, and cream and white.

The bi – colored cat also have a tabby pattern and a
white color is also present like a red tabby and white, or
brown tabby and white. This bi – colors can be found on
both male and female felines.

If a bi – colored feline has more white on it than
color, this is referring to as "bi – color van." The van
pattern is quite common and it can usually be found in bi
– color cats whose color has a tabby or solid pattern. In a
van bi – color pattern, the majority of the color can be
found on the tail and ears.

A cat with a pointed pattern is one that has its pattern and color at the extremities, which includes the ears, feet, face and tail. We may also describe a cat as a color point. There are many people that automatically describe a feline with such pattern as a Siamese cat. Genetically speaking though, the Siamese gene is responsible for this pattern but not every cat with a pointed patter can be considered as a Siamese breed. This pattern is also known as Himalayan pattern, and it has been introduced in various hybrid and non – hybrid breeds as well as at – large gene pool.

Cats that have a pointed pattern may have the following colors:

- Seal Point
- Chocolate Point
- Blue Point
- Red Point
- Lilac Point
- Cream Point
- Seal Tabby Point

- Blue Tabby Point
- Lilac Tabby Point
- Red Tabby Point
- Cream Tabby Point
- Blue – Cream Point
- Tortie Point
- Lilac Tortie or Chocolate Tabby Point

Cats also occur with tipped and shaded colors. The hairs on these felines are white at the roots. At the end of each hair, you may see primary colors such as:

- Blue
- Black
- Red
- Cream Chocolate
- Lilac
- Tortoiseshell
- Blue - Cream

Is eye color associated to the pattern or coat of the cat?

The eye colors of felines have a very wide range. The main colors usually include the following:

- Copper
- Blue – green
- Blue
- Orange
- Hazel
- Yellow
- Green

The pupil of felines is always black. Eye color can be associated with the color of the cat's coat but this doesn't always occur. Most eye color that is linked with a specific coat color does so because of many years of selective breeding. It's only in breeds that were influenced by the Siamese and Burmese gene has the eye color controlled in a genetic way. For the Burmese gene, it is yellow and for the Siamese gene, it is blue.

The mink - patterned tonkinese usually have aqua eyes. This is a hybrid of a Siamese and a Burmese breed.

There are various breeds that do have different requirements for eye color. For instance, Egyptian Mau cat have green eyes, specifically a gooseberry green version as must have for Oriental Shorthair felines and Havana Brown cats.

Predominantly white or white cats can have copper eyes, blue eyes, or one eye of each color – a copper and a blue. If the cat has two then different eye colors, experts call them odd – eyed felines.

Putting It All Together

Usually when an expert is describing a cat, they say the color of the coat first, the next is the pattern, the next is coat length, and the last is the other special features of the breed.

The breed name is usually added at the end of the whole description. So for instance, some will say, "this cat is a red mackerel tabby and white Maine Coon cat." Another example is. "this breed is a sable Burmese," "blue – cream spotted short – hair American Curl," or this one is a seal tortie lynx point Colorpoint Shorthair.

I know this sounds all confusing, and you're right about that because even experts are confused from time to time. Don't worry though because if you acquired a kitten or cat from a legit breeder, you will see the color and pattern on the registration papers. You can then work with your breeder to understand the meaning behind the description.

Those felines with the heaviest amount of pigmentation are called smokes while those who have the least are known as chinchilla. If a cat has a shaded silver coat then that means that the amount of pigmentation falls between the amounts of chinchilla and smoke.

Long and Short Coat Mutations

Coat length can be classified in two major types: long and short. A shorthaired feline usually have a close – lying, dense and plushy coat. In any event, one can easily identify a shorthair cat.

On the other hand, a longhaired cat has a flowing and long coat. It usually drapes and moves with every step. This is the kind of coat that you can see in the top show Persian. It's also important to note that there are variations of the long coat which is known as the intermediate length coat. This is a type that's somewhere between a short and long coat, though it's not really short. Examples of this type include the Turkish Angora, the Maine Coon Cat and the Birman cat.

When referring to the length of a cat or kitten, it's most common to identify it as either longhaired or shorthaired. This is also important as there are breeds that have both longhaired and shorthaired divisions, and they are usually judged separately in cat shows. This includes Scottish Fold cats, Oriental cats, American curls and the likes.

Several Rex genes have also occurred in the past few years. These genes usually cause the coat to become curly. It is in fact linked with the Cornish Rex which causes the guard hair to be absent. The gene in association with the Devon Rex breed allows 3 hairs to be present, while the gene related to the Selkirk Rex also allow 3 hairs but one is a dominant gene while others are recessive. Another coat gene which is known as the American Wirehair also allows the presence of 3 hairs but the hairs are usually all curled in an abnormal fashion, making the texture of the coat stiffer and less soft.

Showing Your Tabby

In cat shows, judges compare cats to breed standards. These standards state how an ideal Tabby cat looks and behaves. Cats score higher when they are able to fulfill more breed standards set by the organizer so make sure that you follow the official breed standards mentioned in the previous section.

Breed standards are accurate, yet flexible. According to the Cat Fanciers Association, the given standards aim to describe features that come from the natural style of the breed, but at times, judges also consider the proportion of the cat's overall features rather than whether they exactly conform to the measurements stated. You can sign up your pet for either a specialty cat shows or an all – breed cat shows. The former is a competition where cats compete within a particular breed or color divisions while the latter is a show that competes with other cat breeds and not just among Tabby.

In the CFA, separate shows run simultaneously throughout a hall, with rings for each judge. The process involves keepers finding their designated cage numbers and waiting to be called. Once the number is called, you can bring your pet to the cages in the different rings where the judges can inspect and rate them.

Don't worry because ring clerks and ring stewards are there to help you out, records are maintained and cages are kept clean. Each judge is also accompanied by a master clerk. After examining all the cats in the all - breed or specialty shows, the judges will then tally the scores and present the top 10 cats. As for the recognition and awarding, there are 1st, 2nd, and 3rd placers but when a cat obtains six ribbons in the open category, it is declared as the champion and proceeds to compete with other champions. Depending on the organization, champion cats that earn 200 points will be declared as the grand champion.

Training Your Tabby Cat for Show

One important thing to keep in mind is not be harsh when you are training your pet. Sure be competitive but not to the point where you will punish your cat if he/ she doesn't cooperate with you. What you can do is use rewards to encourage your cat during training time and always be patient to obtain desirable behavior. Cat show judges inspect not only how your entry looks, but also how it behaves and responds. Training your pet Tabby before a show could be of great help in earning better scores in the judges' books.

One of the first things you need to teach your cat is to stand erect with a good posture. Although it is more difficult to teach cats to sit and stand than dogs, try to train your pet to do these for a few moments. The judges will be impressed. Reward your cat with gentle nose strokes downward whenever it is in good posture. Or you can also ask an expert to train your cat prior to a show. You can also check out the mentorship program of the CFA where newbie keepers can be accustomed to the process in cat shows.

Make sure to play with your cat and offer it treats to keep it as happy and relaxed as possible especially during the show. You can also choose to bring your cat out to a show even if he/she isn't joining yet, so that your Tabby will be familiar with the sights and sounds of the event.

Below are other training tips that your cat needs to get used to:

- Get your cat used to being carried around. Your pet needs to get used to being carried on your forearms and hands. This can be a bit tricky for Tabby cats because they don't want to be carried around much unlike other cat breeds but the earlier you start carrying them comfortably, the better they will feel once the show day arrives.

- Make your Tabby confident by placing them on unfamiliar surfaces. This can include a desk or even on the grooming table. Play with them to make them feel confident being in these surfaces. You can also find a toy that your pet likes and teach it to jump up to touch the toy.

- Keep your pet socialized. Make sure to constantly introduce and socialize your pet to new people and friends so that it does not develop a shy or easily frightened attitude.

Chapter Seven: Health and Nutrition

After you've provided all the "cat essentials," the next thing to keep in mind is their nutrition. Maintaining proper nutrition for your Tabby is one of the most important yet complex aspects of cat ownership. Oftentimes, keepers don't understand how much diet affects a cat's behavior, health, and even longevity. Never neglect proper feeding schedules and amounts of water intake. As a responsible keeper, it's your duty to make sure that their food intake is controlled. Proper nutrition for this breed is essential for their overall health and heart development. There are certain types of food that can be good and bad for them.

What to Feed Tabby Cats?

Feline pets just like humans also need a healthy diet to thrive. Feeding your Tabby cat the wrong food could definitely lead to a health disaster. Knowing the proper amount needed by your pet is best determined by your veterinarian. If you've already bought some cat food but are not sure if it is good for your cat, bring the cat food to your vet to have its nutritional values assessed. Cats whether they are kittens or adults need a balance amount of minerals, vitamins, protein, enzymes, fatty acids and water.

First stop is the most important of all – water. Cats have low levels of thirst because they can fulfill much of their water requirements by eating fresh, raw food. This is why cats that eat dry food often have more health issues than those who eat wet cat food. Cats that lack water in their body end up getting dehydrated and usually have urine that is too concentrated. Make sure to always prepare fresh and clean drinking water for your pet. And if ever you feel that they are not drinking enough, you can get cat drinking fountains that mimic the experience of drinking from running water.

Every cat needs a great amount of protein in their body. Your pet can get a good supply of this from meat since plant sources do not supply Taurine which is an essential amino acid that cats need. If your cat lacks Taurine, this can lead to health issues so make sure to include protein - rich food in their diet. Another important nutrient is vitamins. It is important to household pets as it is for us humans. Vitamins provide good metabolism and also contributes to normal growth and bodily functions.

Another important nutrient that your cat needs on a daily basis is essential fatty acids. This nutrient can't be gain from plant sources, which again justifies why a cat's diet needs to be composed of meat. These nutrients are involved with metabolism functions and cell integrity in a cat's body. Another essential is antioxidants and enzymes can be found in healthy food sources for cats as these can help protect their body from free radicals that can damage the cells.

Last but not the least are minerals are involved in most of a cat's physiological reactions like enzyme formulation, oxygen transportation, and nutrient utilization.

Reminders When Feeding Your Cat

Feeding your pet dry cat food is okay, as long as it is balanced. It could be better to ration the food rather than to free - feed. If your cat only eats dry food, make sure to encourage it to drink much water to avoid developing kidney stones. On the other hand wet food or canned food is always a good choice, but make sure to exercise control over the amount your cat eats since this type of food is more palatable than dry food, this can cause our cat to overeat.

According to veterinarians, mixing dry and wet food to make meals more appealing is not bad. However, you got to make sure that you don't go over the ideal calorie intake of your cat. Make sure to consult your vet for the right amount of food intake.

When it comes to toxic food, some human foods are toxic to cats. This include chocolates and drinks especially with caffeine, dairy products such as butter and milk, garlic , onion, raw dough, alcohol, raisins, grapes, dog food and the likes.

When it comes to frequency of meals, you'd be surprised to know that kittens need more food for development than adult cats. Usually, kittens up to 6 months of age may require being fed 3 meals per day, while most cats over 6 months of age will do fine with just 2 meals per day. Once your cat reaches 7 years old, you may feed them once a day and maintain that routine.

Homemade food is an option by pet owners to make sure that the cat will have adequate water and you will have full control over all of the things you will put there. On the other hand, if you are a very busy person, the conventional commercial premium food is often convenient and often cheaper. The choice heavily relies on your preference. However, if you give raw meat, the risk is that meat might contain parasites that will be harmful to your pet's body. On the other hand, cooked meat will lose some of its nutrients because of the processing. We highly recommend that you could try a combination of the two.

Annual Check – Up for Your Tabby

The health of your Tabby cat is perhaps the most important thing you need to focus on because this will give you benefits in the long run. Think about it, if your pet is healthy, you don't need to pay for medical bills and you will also save time and effort of constantly taking vet trips. You will also save your cat from pain and you're going to lessen the risk of them catching any major illnesses.

However, keep in mind that good health comes with a price. You need to provide the needed vaccines, spay/ neuter them, maintain their hygiene through grooming and go for vet routine checkups to ensure that your cat is at its best health.

When it comes to annual vaccinations, as costly as it may sound, you need to vaccine your cat especially when you got it in a very young stage. Remember, the mother may have given antibodies to prevent common diseases, but these are not enough. Your cat needs additional protection against common ailments.

At around six to eight weeks old, core vaccines are needed, especially for feline distemper, feline calicivirus, and feline rhinotracheitis. You also need to ask your vet if you need to have a vaccine against chlamydia. The core vaccines must be given every three to four weeks, and the final kitten vaccinations should be given at 14 to 16 weeks of age. At around ten to twelve weeks old, second vaccinations of the core vaccines are required.

You may also ask your vet about the feline leukaemia. Then when your pet hits twelve to sixteen weeks old you should already have your pet rabies shot. Third round of vaccination of core vaccines are needed for fourteen to sixteen weeks old kittens.

As for vet exams, they usually like to perform the examination in their own ways, especially with the parts that they are examining. It doesn't matter where they begin, as long as they will examine everything. Remember, this vet examination is done every time you go to the vet. When you schedule your pet for a vet exam, what you can do to help during the process is to calm down your Tabby or keep him/her quiet during a physical examination, especially when the vet is using a stethoscope. Talking during the examination will lead to interruption of your vet's concentration and could interfere with the thoroughness.

You can also ask questions and suggestions after the cat's examination. Questions like if you need to examine your cat at home, what signs are you looking for when examining the cat, how to tell if your cat is overweight or underweight, and what solutions can be done to alleviate the health issue if any can be helpful for you.

Health – Related Threats

Quarantining your pet is needed if you are going to travel overseas or if your pet will be placed in the cargo of the plane or ship along with other animals. Consider the risk for your cat's health and take the necessary steps to ensure that your Tabby is safe and secure.

The concern of many countries with pets from overseas is the transmission of certain diseases. They are afraid that avian influenza and rabies might spread from birds to humans. Rabies is the main concern for cats and other household pets which is why you need to present a rabies vaccination to make sure that your cat does not have rabies.

In addition to this, you need to research how long the quarantine is for the country or place that you will go to. Keep in mind that you will not be with your pet during this quarantine period. A problem for this is the expensiveness of the quarantine, which could last up to six months. Aside from this, there are strict import requirements for pet imports for specific countries.

You also need to think about the possible health threats for your pets when it travels overseas. There is no specific immunization against the avian flu or other dangerous disease or parasites that may affect your pet.

FLUTD

Feline Lower Urinary Tract Disease, or the FLUTD, has a lot of conditions that can affect your cat's urethra and bladder. The symptoms for this disease are not using the litter box, straining even if not producing urine. Aside from this, your cat may also excessively lick its genital area, and there is blood present in the urine. If you ever see these symptoms, make sure to contact your vet immediately.

This could be a painful sign of urethral blockage, which could be fatal in the long run. The major culprit for this disease is infection, cancer, bladder stones, and urinary tract blockage. The treatment for this disease will involve antibiotics, removal of the blockage, and pain medication. Your vet may even suggest a change of diet and increase of water intake to prevent other problems.

Fleas

Fleas are very common disease of your cat. These are parasites that will feed of the blood of your pet. Some early signs that your cat has fleas are hair loss, scratching, and bald patches, especially to those places where your cat has licked excessively.

You may also see the flea eggs, fleas, or flea excretion in your Tabby cat's fur. The treatment to stop this problem is applying a product specially designed to kill fleas and prevent egg development. You need to be sure that you use flea - control products that are especially designed for cats, not those for dogs. Remember, cats are very sensitive to insecticide and a wrong product could potentially kill your beloved Tabby cat.

Dental Problems

Some symptoms for your cat's dental disease will often involve difficulty in eating, change in chewing, and even bad breath. Your cat's bad breath will indicate digestive problems or gingivitis. Other signs of the problem will involve discoloration, red or swollen gums, ulcer on the tongue or gums, loose teeth, constant pawing at the mouth area, and excessive drooling. These things could affect your cat greatly.

If you think your cat has dental problems, you need to take it the vet dentist immediately. He or she will suggest good oral hygiene, brushing the cat's teeth with a toothbrush and toothpaste that is especially made for cats, and giving a new chew toy for exercising, and removing tartar before it hardens up.

Heart Problems and Obesity

This is a common cat health issue that cats face today; this will include a number of ailments such as liver problems, joint pain, and diabetes. You should be able to feel your Tabby cat's ribs and backbones without pressing too hard, especially those with a healthy diet. Aside from this, you can see a discernible waist between the hips and lower ribs. When you view the cat from the side, you should see the tuck in between the tummy, lower ribs, and hips.

These are just some of the common diseases that your cat may face over the course of their life. Be aware and make sure you know the signs that may affect your cat's health. Knowing these things will arm you with enough knowledge on what to do next when these things happen.

Glossary of Cat Terms

Abundism – Referring to a cat that has markings more prolific than is normal.

Acariasis – A type of mite infection.

ACF – Australian Cat Federation

Affix – A cattery name that follows the cat's registered name; cattery owner, not the breeder of the cat.

Agouti – A type of natural coloring pattern in which individual hairs have bands of light and dark coloring.

Ailurophile – A person who loves cats.

Albino – A type of genetic mutation which results in little to no pigmentation, in the eyes, skin, and coat.

Allbreed – Referring to a show that accepts all breeds or a judge who is qualified to judge all breeds.

Alley Cat – A non-pedigreed cat.

Alter – A desexed cat; a male cat that has been neutered or a female that has been spayed.

Amino Acid – The building blocks of protein; there are 22 types for cats, 11 of which can be synthesized and 11 which must come from the diet (see essential amino acid).

Anestrus – The period between estrus cycles in a female cat.

Any Other Variety (AOV) – A registered cat that doesn't conform to the breed standard.

ASH – American Shorthair, a breed of cat.

Back Cross – A type of breeding in which the offspring is mated back to the parent.

Balance – Referring to the cat's structure; proportional in accordance with the breed standard.

Barring – Describing the tabby's striped markings.

Base Color – The color of the coat.

Bicolor – A cat with patched color and white.

Blaze – A white coloring on the face, usually in the shape of an inverted V.

Bloodline – The pedigree of the cat.

Brindle – A type of coloring, a brownish or tawny coat with streaks of another color.

Castration – The surgical removal of a male cat's testicles.

Cat Show – An event where cats are shown and judged.

Cattery – A registered cat breeder; also, a place where cats may be boarded.

CFA – The Cat Fanciers Association.

Cobby – A compact body type.

Colony – A group of cats living wild outside.

Color Point – A type of coat pattern that is controlled by color point alleles; pigmentation on the tail, legs, face, and ears with an ivory or white coat.

Colostrum – The first milk produced by a lactating female; contains vital nutrients and antibodies.

Conformation – The degree to which a pedigreed cat adheres to the breed standard.

Cross Breed – The offspring produced by mating two distinct breeds.

Dam – The female parent.

Declawing – The surgical removal of the cat's claw and first toe joint.

Developed Breed – A breed that was developed through selective breeding and crossing with established breeds.

Down Hairs – The short, fine hairs closest to the body which keep the cat warm.

DSH – Domestic Shorthair.

Estrus – The reproductive cycle in female cats during which she becomes fertile and receptive to mating.

Fading Kitten Syndrome – Kittens that die within the first two weeks after birth; the cause is generally unknown.

Feral – A wild, untamed cat of domestic descent.

Gestation – Pregnancy; the period during which the fetuses develop in the female's uterus.

Guard Hairs – Coarse, outer hairs on the coat.

Harlequin – A type of coloring in which there are van markings of any color with the addition of small patches of the same color on the legs and body.

Inbreeding – The breeding of related cats within a closed group or breed.

Kibble – Another name for dry cat food.

Lilac – A type of coat color that is pale pinkish-gray.

Line – The pedigree of ancestors; family tree.

Litter – The name given to a group of kittens born at the same time from a single female.

Mask – A type of coloring seen on the face in some breeds.

Matts – Knots or tangles in the cat's fur.

Mittens – White markings on the feet of a cat.

Moggie – Another name for a mixed breed cat.

Mutation – A change in the DNA of a cell.

Muzzle – The nose and jaws of an animal.

Natural Breed – A breed that developed without selective breeding or the assistance of humans.

Neutering – Desexing a male cat.

Open Show – A show in which spectators are allowed to view the judging.

Pads – The thick skin on the bottom of the feet.

Particolor – A type of coloration in which there are markings of two or more distinct colors.

Patched – A type of coloration in which there is any solid color, tabby, or tortoiseshell color plus white.

Pedigree – A purebred cat; the cat's papers showing its family history.

Pet Quality – A cat that is not deemed of high enough standard to be shown or bred.

Piebald – A cat with white patches of fur.

Points – Also color points; markings of contrasting color on the face, ears, legs, and tail.

Pricked – Referring to ears that sit upright.

Purebred – A pedigreed cat.

Queen – An intact female cat.

Roman Nose – A type of nose shape with a bump or arch.

Scruff – The loose skin on the back of a cat's neck.

Selective Breeding – A method of modifying or improving a breed by choosing cats with desirable traits.

Senior – A cat that is more than 5 but less than 7 years old.

Sire – The male parent of a cat.

Solid – Also self; a cat with a single coat color.

Spay – Desexing a female cat.

Stud – An intact male cat.

Tabby – A type of coat pattern consisting of a contrasting color over a ground color.

Tom Cat – An intact male cat.

Tortoiseshell – A type of coat pattern consisting of a mosaic of red or cream and another base color.

Tri-Color – A type of coat pattern consisting of three distinct colors in the coat.

Tuxedo – A black and white cat.

Unaltered – A cat that has not been desexed.

Index

C

D

E

F

G

H

I

J

K

Photo Credits

Page 1 Photo by user Free – Photos via Pixabay.com,

https://pixabay.com/photos/cat-feline-tabby-domestic-animal-1245673/

Page 6 Photo by user Alexas_Fotos via Pixabay.com,

https://pixabay.com/photos/cat-red-mackerel-tiger-cuddly-1046544/

Page 16 Photo by user rihaij via Pixabay.com,

https://pixabay.com/photos/cat-kitten-cat-baby-young-cats-1064078/

Page 24 Photo by user Freakwave via Pixabay.com,

https://pixabay.com/photos/kitten-british-shorthair-pet-cat-4277076/

Page 33 Photo by user Freakwave via Pixabay.com,

https://pixabay.com/photos/kitten-silver-tabby-cat-4286604/

Page 51 Photo by user rihaij via Pixabay.com,

https://pixabay.com/photos/cat-mieze-kitten-mackerel-tabby-2219446/

Page 61 Photo by user Alexas_Fotos via Pixabay.com,

https://pixabay.com/photos/cat-red-relaxed-rest-cute-3422863/

Page 81 Photo by user rihaij via Pixabay.com,

https://pixabay.com/photos/cat-kitten-mieze-red-mackerel-tabby-1366118/

References

"Cat Coat Colours And Patterns" – Omlet.co.uk

https://www.omlet.co.uk/guide/cats/choosing_the_right_cat_for_you/cat_coat_colours_and_patterns

"Do You Know What a Tabby Cat Really Is?" – WideOpenPets.com

https://www.wideopenpets.com/know-tabby-cat-really/. . . . .

"The 5 Tabby Cat Patterns" – Catster.com

https://www.catster.com/cats-101/tabby-cat

"Facts About Tabby Cats: What You Need To Know About These Kitties – Traits, Health Issues, Price And More" – Catological.com

https://www.catological.com/facts-tabby-cats/

All About Tabby Cats and Their Color Patterns = TheSprucePets.com

https://www.thesprucepets.com/all-about-tabby-cats-552489

"Taking Care of Tabby" – PetHelpful.com

https://pethelpful.com/cats/tabby-cat-care

"Tabby Cat: 5 Tips For Taking Care Of Kittens" - KittenToob.com

https://kittentoob.com/tabby-cat-5-tips-taking-care-kittens/

"Common Genetic and Non – Genetic Tabby Cat Health Problems" = TabbyCatCare.com

https://tabbycatcare.com/

"Take Good Care of Your Tabby Cat. We'll Tell You How" – CatAppy.com

https://catappy.com/how-to-take-care-of-tabby-cat

"Tabby Cats Information" – PetsWorld.in

https://www.petsworld.in/blog/tabby-cats-information.html

"9 Secrets to Keeping Your Indoor Cat Happy" = Vetstreet.com

http://www.vetstreet.com/cats/

"Indoor Tabby Cat Requirements" – TabbyCatCare.com

https://tabbycatcare.com/essential-products-indoor-tabby-cats/